Wiley
CPAexcel®
EXAM REVIEW
FOCUS NOTES
2015

Wiley

CPAexcel®
EXAM REVIEW
2015
FOCUS NOTES

BUSINESS ENVIRONMENT AND CONCEPTS

WILEY

CONTENTS

v

PREFACE

This publication is a comprehensive, yet simplified study program. It provides a review of all the basic skills and concepts tested on the CPA exam, and teaches important strategies to take the exam faster and more accurately. This tool allows you to take control of the CPA exam.

This simplified and focused approach to studying for the CPA exam can be used:

- As a handy and convenient reference manual
- To solve exam questions
- To reinforce material being studied

Included is all of the information necessary to obtain a passing score on the CPA exam in a concise and easy-to-use format. Due to the wide variety of information covered on the exam, a number of techniques are included:

- Acronyms and mnemonics to help candidates learn and remember a variety of rules and checklists
- Formulas and equations that simplify complex calculations required on the exam
- Simplified outlines of key concepts without the details that encumber or distract from learning the essential elements

- Techniques that can be applied to problem solving or essay writing, such as preparing a multiple-step income statement, determining who will prevail in a legal conflict, or developing an audit program
- Pro forma statements, reports, and schedules that make it easy to prepare these items by simply filling in the blanks
- Proven techniques to help you become a smarter, sharper, and more accurate test taker

This publication may also be useful to university students enrolled in Intermediate, Advanced and Cost Accounting; Auditing, Business Law, and Federal Income Tax classes; or Economics and Finance classes.

Good luck on the exam,

Ray Whittington, PhD, CPA

ABOUT THE AUTHOR

Ray Whittington, PhD, CPA, CMA, CIA, is the dean of the Driehaus College of Business at DePaul University. Prior to joining the faculty at DePaul, Professor Whittington was the Director of Accountancy at San Diego State University. From 1989 through 1991, he was the Director of Auditing Research for the American Institute of Certified Public Accountants (AICPA), and he previously was on the audit staff of KPMG. He previously served as a member of the Auditing Standards Board of the AICPA and as a member of the Accounting and Review Services Committee and the Board of Regents of the Institute of Internal Auditors. Professor Whittington has published numerous textbooks, articles, monographs, and continuing education courses.

ABOUT THE CONTRIBUTOR

Kurt Pany, PhD, CPA, is a Professor of Accounting at Arizona State University. His basic and advanced auditing courses provided the basis on which he received the Arizona Society of CPA's Excellence in Teaching Award and an Arizona CPA Foundation Award for Innovation in the Classroom for the integration of computer and professional ethics applications. His professional experience includes serving for four years on the AICPA's Auditing Standards Board, serving as an academic fellow in the Auditing Division of the AICPA, and prior to entering academe, working as a staff auditor for Deloitte and Touche.

CORPORATE GOVERNANCE AND ENTERPRISE RISK MANAGEMENT

Corporate Governance: Establish Incentives and Monitoring

- Owners separate from management
- Agency problem: Will managers act in owners' interest?

Incentives to Defeat Agency Problem

Forms of Executive Compensation

- Base salary and profit: Usually based on accounting measures
  - May lead to earnings manipulation or taking excessive risk

Focus on

Corporate Governance, Internal Control, and Enterprise Risk Management—Module 40

Incentives to Defeat Agency Problem (continued)

- Stock options: align shareholders' and managers' interest in increasing share prices
  - Differences in timing horizons (management short term?)
  - Underwater options provide no incentive
- Restricted stock: force managers to think long term

Monitoring Devices

- Boards of directors
  - Independent nominating/corporate governance committee
  - Independent audit committee (AC) under Sarbanes-Oxley (SOX)
    - At least one financial expert
    - External auditors must report directly to AC
    - AC appoints, determines compensation, and oversees external auditor

Focus on

**Corporate Governance, Internal Control, and
Enterprise Risk Management—Module 40**

Incentives to Defeat Agency Problem *(continued)*

- Stock exchange rules

  - Majority independent directors

    - Provide information to investors as to who is independent

  - Have and make available code of conduct
  - Have an independent AC (required by SOX)
  - Have an independent compensation committee (required by Dodd-Frank)
  - Clawback rules that require executives to pay back incentive compensation when there is an accounting restatement (required by Dodd-Frank)
  - Nonbinding shareholder votes on executive compensation and golden parachutes (required by Dodd-Frank)

Incentives to Defeat Agency Problem (continued)

- Internal auditors

  - Provide assurance on risk management and internal control

  - Should report at least indirectly to AC

    - Independent and competent

    - Chief IC officer reports directly to CEO

    - Should adhere to Institute of Internal Auditors (IIA) professional and ethical standards. These standards apply to both individual auditors and internal audit departments.

- External auditors

  - Help assure users that financials are accurate and not fraudulent

  - Must attest to management's assessment of effective internal control as required by SOX

  - The Jumpstart Our Business Startups (JOBS) Act exempted "emerging growth companies" for a maximum of five years from the date of their initial public offering from certain requirements that apply to larger public companies, including external reporting on internal control

Incentives to Defeat Agency Problem (continued)

- SEC and SOX

  - CEO and CFO must certify accuracy and truthfulness with criminal penalties
  - Fraud in sale or purchase of securities punishable by fine and/or prison
  - Destruction or other damage to documentation to hinder investigation punishable by fine and/or prison
  - Retaliation on "whistleblowers" punishable by fine and/or prison

Focus on

Corporate Governance, Internal Control, and Enterprise Risk Management—Module 40

Internal Controls

COSO: Internal Control Integrated Framework (Revised 2013)

Internal control is defined by COSO as a process, effected by the entity's board of directors, management, and other personnel, designed to provide reasonable assurance regarding the achievement of objectives relating to operations, reporting, and compliance. It has five components and 16 principles.

1. The **control environment** is the set of standards, processes, and structures that provide the basis for carrying out internal control across the organization. Principles include:

    a. Commitment to integrity and ethical values.

    b. The board of directors demonstrates independence from management and exercises oversight.

    c. Management establishes structures, reporting lines, and appropriate authorities and responsibilities in the pursuit of objectives.

    d. Commitment to attract, develop and retain competent individuals.

    e. Hold individuals accountable for their internal control responsibilities.

Internal Controls (continued)

2. **Risk assessment** is management's process for identifying, analyzing, and responding to risks. Principles include:

   a. Specify objectives with sufficient clarity to enable the identification and assessment of risks.

   b. Identify risks to the achievement of its objectives and analyze risks as a basis for determining how the risks should be managed.

   c. Consider the potential for fraud.

   d. Identify and assesses changes that could significantly impact internal control.

3. **Control activities** are policies and procedures that help ensure that management directives are carried out. Principles include:

   a. Select and develop control activities that contribute to the mitigation of risks.

   b. Select and develop general control activities over technology to support the achievement of objectives.

   c. Deploy control activities through policies that establish what is expected and in procedures that put policies into action.

Internal Controls (continued)

Control activities to mitigate risks include:

a. Authorizations and approvals

b. Verifications

c. Physical controls

d. Controls over standing data

e. Reconciliations

f. Supervisory controls

Focus on

**Corporate Governance, Internal Control, and
Enterprise Risk Management—Module 40**

Internal Controls (continued)

4. The **information and communication** component of internal control supports all of the other components. Principles include:

   a. The organization obtains or generates and uses relevant, quality information to support the functioning of internal control.

   b. The organization internally communicates information, including objectives and responsibilities for internal control.

   c. The organization communicates with external parties regarding matters affecting the functioning of internal control.

5. **Monitoring activities** assess whether each of the five components is present and functioning. Principles include:

   a. Select, develop, and perform ongoing and/or separate evaluations to ascertain whether the components of internal control are present and functioning.

   b. Evaluate and communicate internal control deficiencies in a timely manner to those parties responsible for taking corrective action.

Focus on

**Corporate Governance, Internal Control, and
Enterprise Risk Management—Module 40**

Internal Controls (continued)

Monitoring may be considered as consisting of the following sequence of activities (monitoring for change control continuum):

- **Control baseline**—Establishing a starting point that includes a supported understanding of the existing internal control system.

- **Change identification**—Identifying through monitoring changes in internal control that are either necessary because of changes in the operating environment or have already taken place.

- **Change management**—Evaluating the design and implementation of the changes, and establishing a new baseline.

- **Control revalidation/update**—Periodically revalidating control operation when no known changes have occurred.

Enterprise Risk Management: Eight Components

1. Internal environment (tone of the organization)

    a. Effective board

    b. Ethical management

    c. Risk appetite: How much risk is organization willing to accept to achieve a goal?

    d. Risk tolerance: How far above or below meeting objective is allowable?

2. Objective setting

    a. Well-defined mission

    b. Process to set objectives that align with goals

3. Event identification

    a. Internal

        1) Loss of key personnel

        2) Damage to infrastructure (e.g., IS crash)

        3) Key product/process becomes obsolete

Focus on

**Corporate Governance, Internal Control, and
Enterprise Risk Management—Module 40**

Enterprise Risk Management: Eight Components (continued)

    b. External

        1) Establish "trigger points" (e.g., competition increases market share above x amount)

        2) Process to assess demographic and economic changes

    c. Black swan analysis: Evaluate negative events that were unforeseen to determine why

4. Risk assessment: What are the risks?

    a. Assess impact and probability

    b. Inherent risk: What if management does nothing in response to identified risk?

    c. Residual risk: residual after management's response

Focus on

**Corporate Governance, Internal Control, and
Enterprise Risk Management—Module 40**

Enterprise Risk Management: Eight Components (continued)

5. Risk responses

   a. Avoidance

   b. Reduction

   c. Sharing

   d. Acceptance

6. Control activities: Policies and procedures to insure that risk responses are implemented

7. Information and communication throughout organization

   a. Organization's objectives

   b. Risk appetite and tolerance

   c. Role of ERM in managing risk

8. Monitoring: Effective process to oversee ERM

Focus on

Corporate Governance, Internal Control, and Enterprise Risk Management—Module 40

Enterprise Risk Management: Limitations

1. The future is uncertain
2. No absolute assurances
   a. Human failure
   b. System breakdown
   c. Collusion across ERM
   d. Management override

INFORMATION TECHNOLOGY

Attributes of Paper versus Electronic Systems

Difficulty of alteration—It is easier to change electronic data without detection

Prima facie credibility—The origin of paper documents is easier to determine

Completeness of documents—Paper documents typically include more information than electronic documents

Evidence of approvals—Paper documents show approvals more obviously

Ease of use—Electronic data requires specialized knowledge to be accessed by the auditor

Benefits of IT

Consistency—Computers process data the same way every time.

Timeliness—Electronic processing and updating is normally more efficient.

Analysis—Data can be accessed for analytical procedures more conveniently (with proper software).

Monitoring—Electronic controls can be monitored by the computer system itself.

Circumvention—Controls are difficult to circumvent when programmed properly, and exceptions are unlikely to be permitted.

Risks of IT

Overreliance—Without clear output, IT systems are often assumed to be working when they are not.

Access—Destruction and alteration of large amounts of data are possible if unauthorized access occurs.

Changes in programs—Severe consequences without detection are possible if unauthorized program changes occur.

Failure to change—Programs are sometimes not updated for new laws, rules, or activities.

Manual intervention—Knowledgeable individuals can sometimes alter files by bypassing the appropriate programs.

Loss of data—Catastrophic data loss is possible if appropriate controls aren't in place.

Systems Design and Process Improvement

A Seven-Step Process (PADDTIM)

1. Planning
   a. Define system to be developed
   b. Determine project scope
   c. Develop project plan
2. **Analysis**
   a. Meet with users and IS staff
   b. Conduct needs assessment of users
   c. Conduct gap analysis between needs and existing systems
3. **Design** (technical blueprint of new system)
4. **Development: Build**
   a. Platform
   b. Software

A Seven-Step Process (PADDTIM) (continued)

5. Testing
   a. Unit tests (pieces of code)
   b. System tests (Do units within a system integrate?)
   c. Integration testing (Do separate systems integrate?)
   d. User acceptance
6. Implementation: several strategies
   a. Parallel implementation: run old and new
   b. Plunge: Stop old, use new
   c. Pilot
   d. Phased
7. Maintenance
   a. Monitor and support
      1) Training
      2) Help desk
      3) Process and policies for authorizing changes

Focus on

Information Technology—Module 41

Hardware

Hardware is the actual electronic equipment. Common components include:

- **Central processing unit** or **CPU**—The principal hardware component that processes programs

- **Memory**—The internal storage space or **online storage**, often referred to as **random access memory** or **RAM**

- **Offline storage**—Devices used to store data or programs externally, including floppy disks, magnetic tape, digital video discs (DVDs), and compact discs (CDs)

- **File server**—A computer with a large internal memory used to store programs and data that can be accessed by all workstations in the network

- **Input and output devices**—Devices that allow for communication between the computer and users and for the storage of data, such as a terminal with a screen and a keyboard, scanners, microphones, wireless handheld units, barcode readers, point-of-sale registers, optical character readers, mark sense readers, light guns, printers, speakers, CD and DVD drives, magnetic tape drives, and magnetic disk drives

Size and Power of Computers

Hardware comes in various sizes, depending on the volume and complexity of users' needs. In declining order of power, computer hardware includes:

- **Supercomputers**—Common for massive scale needs by science and math departments of universities and large governmental operations

- **Mainframe computers**—Until recently, often the only computer a large organization might have, with several terminals having the ability to connect to it simultaneously

- **Minicomputers**—Until recently, a less expensive alternative to mainframes used by smaller organizations as their primary computer with accessibility through multiple terminals

- **Microcomputers**—Personal computers designed for use by a single individual, including desktops and laptops

- **Personal digital assistants**—Handheld computers with limited processing capabilities that normally emphasize easy connection and transfer of data with the primary microcomputer used by an individual

Focus on

Information Technology—Module 41

Storage Devices

Magnetic tape—Inexpensive form of storage used primarily for backup, since only **sequential** access of data is possible.

Magnetic disks—Permanent storage devices inside a computer (including hard drives) that allow **random** access to data without the need to move forward or backward through all intervening data. Some systems use **RAID** (redundant array of independent disks), which includes multiple disks in one system so that data can be stored redundantly and the failure of one of the disks won't cause the loss of any data.

Removable disks—Transportable forms of storage. In increasing order of capacity, these include:

- Compact discs (CDs)
- Optical discs (DVDs)

Data Entry Devices

Visual display terminal (keyboard and monitor)

Mouse (including joystick and light pen)

Touch-sensitive screen

Magnetic tape reader

Magnetic ink character reader

Scanner

Automatic teller machine

Radio frequency data communication

Point-of-sale register

Voice recognition

Electronic data interchange

Focus on

Information Technology—Module 41

Software

Software is either system software or application software.

- **System software** is made up of the programs that run the system and direct its operations. It is comprised of the operating system and utility programs

- **Utility** programs are used for sorts, merges, and other routine functions to maintain and improve the efficiency of a computer system

- **Communication software** handles transmission of data between different computers

- Specialized **security software** is a type of utility program used to control access to the computer or its files

Programming languages:

- **Source program** is in the language written by the programmer (high-level languages resemble English while assembly languages are closer to direct machine instructions)

- **Object program** is in a form the machine understands (on-off or 1-0)

- **Compiler** is a program that converts source programs into machine language

Data Structure

Bit—A single switch in a computer that is either in the on (1) or off (0) position

Byte—A group of eight bits representing a character

Character—A letter, number, punctuation mark, or special character

Alphanumeric—A character that is either a letter or number

Field—A group of related characters representing a unit of information (such as a phone number or a city name)

Record—A group of logically related fields (such as the name, address, and telephone of one employee)

File—A group of logically related records (such as the contact information for all the employees)

- Master file—A permanent source that is used as an ongoing reference and that is periodically updated
- Detail file—A file listing a group of transactions that can be used to update a master file

Types of Computer Systems

Transaction processing systems—General record keeping and reporting needs

Management reporting systems—Assist in decision making within the organization

- **Management information system**—Provides information to management, which may utilize it in decision making

- **Decision support system**—Combines models and data to help in problem solving but with extensive user interpretation needed

- **Expert system**—Uses reasoning methods and data to render advice and recommendations in structured situations where human interpretation isn't necessary

- **Executive information system**—Systems designed specifically to support executive work

Focus on

Information Technology—Module 41

The Accounting Process in an IT Environment

The two primary approaches to the processing of data are batch processing and online processing.

1. **Batch processing**—Input data is collected over a period of time and processed periodically

2. **Online processing**—Individuals originating transactions process them from remote locations in a batch, similar to batch processing, or immediately in an **online, real-time system**

Online, real-time systems update accounting records immediately as transactions occur, but result in significant changes in internal control.

- Source documents are often not available to support input into the computer
- The audit trail is usually significantly reduced, requiring controls programmed into the computer

Focus on

Information Technology—Module 41

Electronic Commerce

Electronic commerce using **electronic data interchange** or **EDI** adds to the complexity of auditing. EDI enables:

- Communication without the use of paper
- Electronic funds transfers and sales over the Internet
- Simplification of the recording process using scanning devices
- Sending information to trading partners as transactions occur

EDI transactions are formatted using strict standards that have been agreed to worldwide, often requiring companies to acquire translation software.

Risks of E-Commerce

Electronic commerce increases the risk of improper use of information. Controls might include:

- Data encryption
- Controls to prevent electronic eavesdropping

There is also the risk of improper distribution of transactions with information being electronically transmitted to an inappropriate company. Controls might include:

- Routing verification procedures
- Message acknowledgement procedures

The reduction in the paper audit trail associated with EDI creates special challenges to the auditor.

- Detection risk may not be sufficiently reduced through substantive testing
- Control risk must be reduced adequately to achieve an acceptable level of audit risk
- Controls must be built into the system to insure the validity of information captured

Focus on

Information Technology—Module 41

Networks

In a computer network, computers are connected to one another to enable sharing of peripheral devices, sharing data and programs stored on a **file server**, and communicating with one another.

Networks allow various user departments to share information files maintained in **databases**. Databases should:

- Provide departments with information that is appropriate
- Prevent access to inappropriate information

A company may create its own **value-added network** or **VAN**.

- A **local area network** (**LAN**) is used when computers are physically near to one another
- A **wide area network** (**WAN**) uses high-speed, long-distance communications networks or satellites to connect computers that are not near to one another

Cloud computing is the use and access of multiple server-based computational resources via a digital network (WAN, Internet connection using the World Wide Web, etc.)

The Internet

The **Internet** is a worldwide network that allows virtually any computer system to link to it by way of an electronic gateway. The Internet facilitates data communication services including:

- Remote login
- File transfer
- Electronic mail
- Newsgroups
- Videoconferencing
- Groupware systems

Intranets use Internet technology in closed networks.

Extranets use Internet technology to link businesses with suppliers, customers, and others.

Networks are part of a decentralized processing system applying **distributed data processing.** Users share programs, peripheral devices, and data.

In **client/server computing,** smaller programs are distributed to the workstations, enabling the user to communicate with the network. This is referred to as front-end processing.

In **end user computing,** a user department generates and uses its own information.

The Internet (continued)

To make use of the Internet more user-friendly, a framework for accessing documents was developed, known as the World Wide Web

- **Hypertext Transfer Protocol (HTTP)**—The language commonly understood by different computers to communicate via the Internet
- **Document**—A single file on any computer that is accessible through the Internet
- **Page**—The display that results from connection to a particular document on the Internet
- **Uniform Resource Locator (URL)**—The "address" of a particular page on the Internet
- **Web browser**—A program that allows a computer with a particular form of operating software to access the Internet and that translates documents for proper display
- **Server**—The computer that is "sending" the pages for display on another computer
- **Client**—The computer that is "receiving" the pages and seeing the display
- **Upload**—Sending information from a client to a server computer
- **Download**—Sending information from a server to a client computer

The Internet (continued)

Web 2.0 is a 2nd generation of the web. Refers to era of web-based collaboration and community generated content via web-based software tools such as

- **Blog**—An asynchronous discussion, or web log, led by a moderator that typically focuses on a single topic
- **Wiki**—An information-gathering and knowledge-sharing website that is developed collaboratively by a community or group
- **Twitter**—A micro-variation of a blog. Restricts input (tweets) to 140 characters

Many companies use software to monitor and manage their reputations in social media.

Focus on

Information Technology—Module 41

Networks and Control Risk

To minimize control risk, a network should have some form of security that limits access to certain files to authorized individuals.

- Certain individuals may have read-only access to files
- Others will be authorized to alter the data in the files

A **virus** is a program that requests a computer to perform an activity that is not authorized by the user. A **worm** is a program that duplicates itself over a network so as to infect many computers with viruses.

A tool for establishing security is a **firewall**, which prevents unauthorized users from accessing data.

Control Objectives for Information and Related Technology (COBIT)

COBIT 5 is a framework for integrating IT with business strategy and governance. It incorporates the following five principles:

1. Meeting stakeholder needs
2. Covering the enterprise end-to-end
3. Applying a single integrated framework
4. Enabling a holistic approach
5. Separating governance from management

Control Objectives for Information and Related Technology (COBIT) (continued)

COBIT 5 enablers include:

- Processes—an organized set of practices to achieve objectives
- Organizational structures—the key decision-making entities in an organization
- Culture, ethics, and behavior of individuals and the organization
- Principles, policies and frameworks
- Information produced and used by the enterprise
- Services, infrastructure, and applications
- People, skills, and competencies required for successful completion of activities and making accurate decisions

Organization of an IT Environment

Organization of the IT function is largely dependent on the size of the company and the number of employees involved.

- Larger companies will have a separate IT department
- Others will have many IT functions performed by employees in the accounting department and end users

One characteristic of an IT environment is a reduction in the segregation of duties. Although this might appear to create a potential problem:

- A computer has no incentive to conceal its errors
- Functions can often be combined in an IT environment without weakening internal control

Organization in a Segregated Department

In a well-staffed IT department, systems, operations, and other technical services would be segregated. Each of these segments would be under the supervision of the information systems manager, who might report to the president of the company, one of the vice presidents, or the controller.

Systems Development and Maintenance

Systems might include:

- A **systems analyst** designs the information system using systems flowcharts and other tools and prepares specifications for applications programmers.

- An **application programmer** writes, tests, and debugs programs that will be used in the system. The programmer also develops instructions for operators to follow when running the programs.

- A **database administrator** plans and administers the database to make certain that only appropriate individuals have access to information in it.

Operations in an IT Function

Operations might include data entry, computer operations, program and file librarians, and data control.

- A **data entry clerk** converts data into computer-readable form.
- A **computer operator** runs the programs on the computer.
- **Program and file librarians** are responsible for the custody of computer programs, master files, transaction files, and other records.
- **Data control** is responsible for reviewing and testing input procedures, monitoring processing, and reviewing and distributing outputs.

Focus on

Information Technology—Module 41

Other Technical Services

Other technical services might include telecommunications, systems programming or technical support, and security administration.

- **Telecommunications** is responsible for maintaining and enhancing computer networks and network connections.

- A **systems programmer** or **technical support** is responsible for updating and maintaining the operating systems.

- **Security administration** is responsible for security of the system including control of access and maintenance of user passwords.

Focus on

Information Technology—Module 41

Controls in an IT Environment

As a result of limited segregation of duties and a reduced paper audit trail, the auditor will often have to rely more heavily on the ability to reduce control risk rather than detection risk in order to keep audit risk at an acceptably low level.

The objectives of controls in an IT environment are:

- Completeness
- Accuracy
- Validity
- Authorization
- Timeliness
- Integrity

Controls will include general controls, application controls, input controls, processing controls, and output controls.

General Controls

General controls ensure that the control environment is stable and well managed so that application controls are effective. They relate to personnel policies, file security, contingency planning, computer facilities, and access to computer files.

- **Personnel policies** provide for proper separation of duties and the use of computer accounts that provide users with passwords or other means of preventing unauthorized access.

- **File security policies** safeguard files from accidental or intentional errors or abuse. Security controls involve internal and external file labels, creating backup copies of critical files, lockout procedures, and file protection. These policies also incorporate contingency planning.

- **Hardware controls** are built into the computer equipment to ensure proper functioning, such as **parity checks** that verify all bytes of data are stored as an even number of bits (for even-parity computers) and **echo checks** in which data that is transmitted is sent back to verify that it was received correctly.

Contingency Planning

Unanticipated interruptions are avoided through **contingency planning** that includes fault-tolerant systems and backup files. One approach to backup is the **grandfather-parent-child** procedure in which three generations of files are retained.

A contingency plan will include a **disaster recovery plan** to prepare for the possibility of fires, floods, earthquakes, or terrorist bombings. The plan should specify backup sites to be used for alternate processing.

- A **hot site** is a location that includes a computer system that is already configured similarly to the system regularly used by the company, allowing for immediate use.

- A **cold site** is a location where power and space are available allowing for the installation of processing equipment on short notice.

Controls over **computer facilities** should include locating the facility in a safe place, limiting access to appropriate employees, and maintaining insurance.

Passwords or other forms of identification should be used to limit **access to computer files.**

Application Controls

Application controls include:

- **Preventive controls** are designed to prevent errors and fraud.
- **Detective controls** and **automated controls** are designed to detect errors and fraud.
- **User controls** and **corrective controls** allow individual users to follow up on detected errors and fraud.

In an IT environment, application controls relate to data input, data processing, and data output.

Input Controls

Input controls are designed to ensure the validity, accuracy, and completeness of data entered into the system. Errors can be avoided through:

- Observational controls
- Use of point-of-sale devices, such as scanners, to gather and record data automatically

The use of preprinted recording forms can minimize errors.

Data transcription controls, such as preformatted screens, can minimize errors when converting data to machine-readable form.

Focus on

Information Technology—Module 41

Edit Tests

Edit tests scrutinize data as it is input to determine if it is in an appropriate form. When not in appropriate form, transactions will be rejected and an exception report will be created. Examples include:

- Tests of numeric field content
- Tests of alphabetic field content
- Tests of alphanumeric field content
- Tests for valid codes
- Tests of reasonableness
- Tests of sign
- Tests of completeness
- Tests of sequence
- Tests of consistency

Other input controls include an unfound-record test, a check digit control procedure, or a self-checking digit.

Processing Controls

Once data has been input, processing controls ensure that the data is properly manipulated to produce meaningful output.

- Systems and software documentation allows system analysts to verify that processing programs are complete and thorough

- Computer programs can be tested using error testing compilers to ensure that they do not contain programming language errors

- Test data exposes the program to one sample of each type of exception condition likely to occur during its use

- System testing can be used to make certain that programs within the system are interacting properly

Focus on

Information Technology—Module 41

Output Controls

Output controls ensure that the processing results are valid and monitor the distribution and use of output. The completeness, accuracy, and validity of processing results can be checked using activity listings.

The distribution and use of output can be monitored using numbered forms and, distribution lists and by requiring signatures for certain reports.

When information is particularly sensitive, users might be instructed to use paper shredders to dispose of reports after use.

Control Totals

When data is entered in batches, one way to verify the accuracy of the data is through the use of control totals. Examples are:

- **Record count**—The total number of entries being made (such as the total number of employees being entered into a payroll program)

- **Financial total**—The sum of a column of numbers expressed in dollar form (such as the total value of all the checks)

- **Nonfinancial total**—The meaningful sum of a column of numbers expressed in some type of unit other than dollars (such as the sum of the number of hours worked by the employees)

- **Hash total**—The meaningless sum of a column of numbers (such as the sum of the employee ID numbers)

Controls can immediately verify the accuracy of input or be used to ensure the accuracy of processing calculations or output that is being posted to files. Discrepancies can generate an error message or exception report.

Focus on

Information Technology—Module 41

Controls Over Microcomputers

Microcomputers present additional control risks since they are small and portable, making them easier to steal or damage. Data and software are also more accessible in a microcomputer environment, and individuals can more readily access unauthorized records and modify, copy, or destroy data and software.

A variety of controls can be employed in a microcomputer environment:

- Maintain an inventory listing of all microcomputer equipment and the purposes for which it is used
- Keyboard locks can be built into the CPUs of microcomputers so that unauthorized users will not have access
- Microcomputers and monitors can be secured to desks or fixtures to discourage theft
- Passwords that are changed periodically limit the access of unauthorized users to sensitive data
- Periodic backup of data on microcomputers enables recovery in the case of alteration or destruction of data
- Sensitive information can be maintained in off-line storage kept in locked cabinets to prevent unauthorized access

Flowcharts

Flowcharts diagram the design of internal controls.

Symbols used:

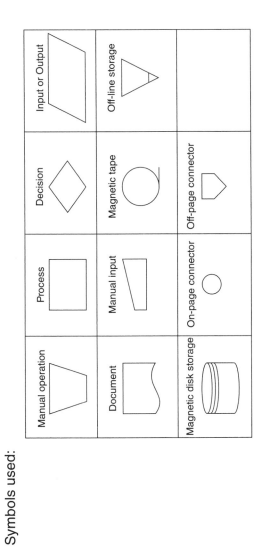

Manual operation	Process	Decision	Input or Output
Document	Manual input	Magnetic tape	Off-line storage
Magnetic disk storage	On-page connector	Off-page connector	

ECONOMIC CONCEPTS

Demand Curve

As the price of a product increases, the quantity demanded by buyers decreases. This is reflected by a demand curve that is plotted with quantity demands on the x-axis (horizontal) and price on the y-axis (vertical):

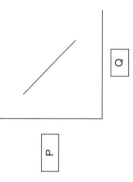

Demand Curve Shifts

When some variables other than the price of the product causes demand to change, it is referred to as a **demand curve shift.**

Positive shift—An increase in demand at each price (the line moves to the right)

Negative shift—A decrease in demand at each price (the line moves to the left)

This is an illustration of a positive demand curve shift:

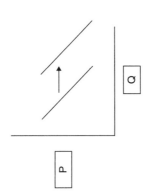

Positive Demand Curve Shift

Certain factors have a **direct** relationship to the demand curve for a product (an increase in that factor will cause the demand curve to have a positive shift to the right):

- **The price of substitute goods**—When another product may be an acceptable alternative, an increase in its price will make the present product more attractive. For example, an increase in the price of hamburgers will cause a positive shift in the demand for hot dogs.

- **Expectations of price increases**—Consumers are more likely to buy now if they think prices will be going up in the future.

- **Consumer income and wealth**—For **normal goods**, the demand will increase if consumers have more wealth to spend on goods.

- **Size of the market**—When new consumers are available to purchase a product, such as when trade barriers between countries are removed, demand for the product will increase.

Negative Demand Curve Shift

Certain factors have an **inverse** relationship to the demand curve for a product (an increase in that factor will cause the demand curve to have a negative shift to the left):

- **The price of complementary goods**—When products are normally used together, an increase in the price of one of the goods harms demand for the other. For example, an increase in the price of hamburgers will cause a negative shift in the demand for hamburger buns.

- **Consumer income and wealth**—For **inferior goods**, the demand will decrease if consumers have more wealth to spend on goods. For example, the demand for tire patches will likely decrease as people become wealthier, since they are more likely to be able to replace the tires rather than patch them.

- **Group boycott**—An organized boycott will, if effective, decrease the demand for a product.

Other factors affect the demand curve in significant but indeterminate ways, such as changes in consumer tastes.

Elasticity of Demand

Price Elasticity = Percentage change in quantity demanded / Percentage change in price

If elasticity is greater than 1, demand is considered **elastic**, and total revenue will decline if the price is increased, since the percentage drop in demand exceeds the percentage increase in price. A firm will be unable to pass on cost increases to consumers in these circumstances.

If elasticity is equal to 1, demand is considered **unitary**, and total revenue will remain the same if the price is increased.

If elasticity is less than 1, demand is considered **inelastic**, and total revenue will increase if the price is increased, since the percentage increase in price exceeds the decrease in demand. A firm will be able to raise prices in these circumstances.

Income Elasticity = Percentage change in quantity demanded / Percentage change in income

This will be a positive number for normal goods and a negative number for inferior goods.

Cross-Elasticity = Percentage change in demand for product X / Percentage change in price of product Y

This will be a positive number for substitute goods and a negative number for complements.

Consumer Demand and Utility

Marginal utility—The satisfaction value to consumers of the next dollar they spend on a particular product.

Law of diminishing marginal utility—The more a consumer has of a particular product, the less valuable will be the next unit of that product. As a result, a consumer maximizes satisfaction when the last dollar spent on each product generates the exact same amount of marginal utility.

Personal disposable income—The available income of a consumer after subtracting payment of taxes or adding receipt of government benefits. The consumer will either spend (consume) or save this income.

Marginal propensity to consume (MPC)—The percentage of the next dollar in personal disposable income that the consumer would be expected to spend.

Marginal propensity to save (MPS)—The percentage of the next dollar in personal disposable income that the consumer would be expected to save (MPC plus MPS must equal 100%, or 1).

Focus on

Economics, Strategy, and Globalization—Module 42

Supply Curve

As the price of a product increases, the quantity offered by sellers increases. This is reflected by a supply curve that is plotted with quantity on the x-axis (horizontal) and price on the y-axis (vertical):

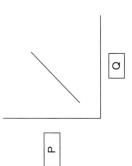

Supply Curve Shifts

When some variable other than the price of the product causes supply to change, it is referred to as a **supply curve shift.**

Positive shift—An increase in supply at each price (the line moves to the right)

Negative shift—A decrease in supply at each price (the line moves to the left)

This is an illustration of a positive supply curve shift:

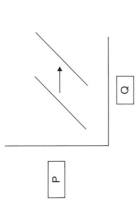

Factors Causing a Supply Curve Shift

Factors with a **direct** relationship on the supply curve include:

- Number of producers
- Government subsidies
- Price expectations

Factors with an **inverse** relationship on the supply curve include:

- Changes in production costs
- Prices of other goods

Market Equilibrium

The price at which the quantity demanded and quantity offered intersect is the equilibrium price:

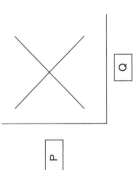

When the government intervenes to impose price ceilings, setting the price below equilibrium, the quantity demanded will exceed quantity offered, resulting in shortages of goods. When the government intervenes to impose price floors, setting price above equilibrium, the quantity offered will exceed quantity demanded, resulting in unsold surpluses of goods.

Short-Run Costs of Production

Over short periods of time and limited ranges of production, costs include **fixed** and **variable** components:

Fixed costs—Costs that won't change even when there is a change in production. Average fixed costs are total fixed costs divided by units produced. An example is rent paid on the production facility.

Variable costs—Costs that will rise as production rises. Average variable costs are total variable costs divided by units produced. An example is materials used in the manufacture of the product.

Total costs—The sum of fixed and variable costs. Average total costs are total costs divided by units produced.

Marginal cost—The increase in cost that will result from an increase in one unit in production. Only variable costs are relevant, since fixed costs won't increase in such circumstances.

Long-Run Costs of Production

In the long run, all costs are variable, since increasing production beyond certain levels will require increases in capacity, causing even "fixed" costs to rise.

Return to scale is the increase in units produced (output) that results from an increase in production costs (input).

Return to scale = Percentage increase in output / Percentage increase in input

When return to scale is greater than 1, we have **increasing returns to scale**. This will normally occur up to a certain level for all firms because of **economies of scale**, or the increased efficiency that results from producing more units of a product (such as the ability to have employees specialize in different tasks and improve their abilities).

When return to scale is less than 1, we have **decreasing returns to scale**. This will normally occur beyond a certain level for all firms because of **diseconomies of scale**, or the increased inefficiencies that result from expanding production (such as the greater difficulty management has in controlling the activities of larger numbers of employees and facilities).

Firms should not increase production beyond levels at which marginal revenue from output exceeds marginal costs from inputs.

Measures of Economic Activity

Gross domestic product (GDP)—The price of all goods and services produced by a domestic economy for a year at current market prices.

Real GDP—GDP adjusted to remove the effect of price inflation in the goods and services. In theory, real GDP growth above a certain level (called **potential GDP**) results in price inflation.

Gross national product (GNP)—The price of all goods and services produced by labor and property supplied by the nation's residents. It differs from GDP in two ways:

1. GNP includes income received by the nation's resident from other countries for products that are a part of foreign economies.

2. GNP excludes payments made to the residents of other countries for products that are a part of the domestic economy.

GDP/GNP may be computed using one of two different approaches:

1. **Income approach**—National income plus depreciation (and a few small adjustments)

2. **Expenditure approach**—Consumption plus private investment plus government purchases (and a few small adjustments)

Aggregate Demand and Supply

Effects of Price Inflation

Just as there are demand and supply curves for individual products, aggregate curves can be depicted for overall prices and production of goods and services of an entire economy. Price inflation will shift the aggregate demand curve for several reasons:

- **Interest rate effect**—Price inflation causes an increase in interest rates and decreases the willingness of consumers to borrow, causing a negative shift in the demand curve for items whose purchase is typically financed, such as houses and automobiles.

- **Wealth effect**—Price inflation causes the value of fixed income investments (such as bonds) to decrease, causing individuals to have less wealth and reducing their consumption of normal goods. (The consumption of inferior goods will increase, but these are typically a small part of the overall economy.)

- **International purchasing power effect**—Domestic price inflation makes domestic goods and services more expensive relative to foreign goods and services, causing an increased demand for foreign products and a negative shift in the demand curve for domestic goods and services.

Focus on

Economics, Strategy, and Globalization—Module 42

Measuring Price Inflation

There are three common measures of price inflation:

1. **Consumer price index (CPI)**—This measures the price of a fixed basket of goods and services that a typical urban consumer might purchase in relation to the price of the same goods and services in an earlier base period.

2. **Producer price index (PPI)**—This measures a fixed basket of goods at the wholesale cost to dealers (such as retail stores) rather than the price to consumers.

3. **GDP deflator**—This utilizes the total production of the economy as measured by GDP and is used to convert GDP to real GDP.

A decline in general price levels is known as **deflation**.

Demand-Pull Inflation

When aggregate spending increases, the **demand** curve moves to the **right**, causing the market equilibrium to occur at higher price levels:

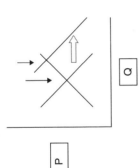

Notice that the equilibrium point occurs at a higher level of prices AND quantity. This is the basis for the historical theory that higher inflation results in higher productivity and, therefore, lower unemployment. The trade-off between inflation and unemployment is known as the **Phillips curve**. Many modern economists reject this theory, or believe that increases in inflation cause only a temporary decline in unemployment.

Focus on

Economics, Strategy, and Globalization—Module 42

Cost-Push Inflation

When production costs increase, the **supply** curve moves to the **left**, causing the market equilibrium to occur at higher price levels:

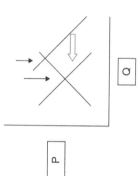

Notice that the equilibrium occurs at a higher level of prices but at a lower quantity. This means that prices are rising but output is declining, usually resulting in higher unemployment. This effect directly contradicts the theory of the Phillips curve.

Multiplier Effect

There will be a positive shift in the demand curve when there is an increase in spending by consumers, businesses, or governments. The size of the shift will be significantly larger than the amount spent, due to the **multiplier effect** of increased spending increasing the income of suppliers, who in turn will spend more, increasing the income of other suppliers, and so on.

The size of the multiplier effect depends on the percentage of increased income that is expected to be spent, or the **marginal propensity to consume**, and the related percentage of increased income that is expected to be saved, or the **marginal propensity to save**. (These two must add up to 1 for the overall economy just as they did for each individual consumer.)

The increase in the equilibrium GDP that results from an injection of new spending is:

Change in spending / Marginal propensity to save

For example, if those making up the economy overall are likely to spend 75% of increased income and save the other 25%, then a change in spending of $100 will raise GDP by $400:

$$\$100 / 25\% = \$400$$

Focus on

Economics, Strategy, and Globalization—Module 42

69

Business Cycle

Expansion—Periods of increased aggregate spending will cause a positive shift in the demand curve to the right and result in a higher equilibrium GDP. Technological advances will cause a positive shift in the supply curve and also result in a higher equilibrium GDP.

Contraction—Periods of decreased aggregate spending will shift the demand curve to the left and result in a lower equilibrium GDP. Trade wars between nations (and wars in general) cause a negative shift in the supply curve and also cause a decline in GDP.

Recession—Two consecutive quarters of negative GDP growth.

Depression—A contraction of GDP that continues for a long period of time. (There is no formal agreement as to the length of time a recession must continue to be called a depression, but it will usually be multiple years.)

Panic—A severe contraction of GDP occurring within a very short time frame (generally lasting less than a year).

Recovery—The term used to refer to the period of expansion that follows the end of a contraction.

Indicators of Business Cycles

Leading indicator—A measure that is being used to try to predict recoveries and recessions. These indicators will normally start moving up months before an actual recovery begins and start moving down months before an actual recession begins. There are many such indicators with variable success in predicting the business cycle. One of the most useful is changes in **stock market prices.**

Coincident indicator—A measure that normally moves up and down simultaneously with economic recoveries and recessions, respectively, and is used to determine if the economy is expanding or contracting at the present time. One example is **industrial production.**

Lagging indicator—A measure that normally starts moving up months after a recovery has begun and starts declining months after a recession has begun. It is used to confirm evidence that the economy has been expanding or contracting over the past few months. A commonly used lagging indicator is the **average prime rate** for bank loans.

Unemployment

The unemployment rate is the percentage of those people who are looking for work who are currently not employed. There are three types of unemployment:

1. **Frictional**—This represents the time period during which people are unemployed as a result of changing jobs or newly entering the workforce. Because of the mobility of society, there is always some level of this type of unemployment, even in a society that effectively has "full" employment.

2. **Structural**—This represents potential workers whose job skills do not match the needs of the workforce as a result of changing demand for goods and services of technological advances that reduce or eliminate the need for the skills they possess. Such unemployment normally requires retraining in order for these individuals to be employable again.

3. **Cyclical**—This represents the unemployment caused by variations in the business cycle, when real GDP fails to grow at the pace necessary to employ all willing workers.

Focus on

Economics, Strategy, and Globalization—Module 42

Interest Rates

This term refers to the price that borrowers must pay for the use of money.

- **Nominal interest rate**—The rate as measured in terms of the nation's currency
- **Real interest rate**—The rate adjusted for inflation
- **Risk-free interest rate**—The rate that would be charged to a borrower if the lender had an absolute certainty of being repaid (The rate paid on United States Treasury securities is often considered to be a useful measure of the risk-free interest rate.)
- **Discount rate**—The rate set by the Federal Reserve System at which a bank can borrow from a Federal Reserve bank
- **Prime rate**—The rate that banks charge their most creditworthy customers on short-term loans from the bank

Government Involvement in the Economy

Fiscal policy—By the manner in which it collects taxes and spends, the government may try to aid certain industries or the economy as a whole. A common technique is known as **fiscal expansion** or **deficit spending**, which involves raising spending levels without an equivalent increase in taxes or lowering taxes without an equivalent decrease in spending. The goal is to increase aggregate spending in the economy and benefit from the multiplier effect.

Monetary policy—The Federal Reserve System (or "Fed") is charged with control over the money supply. By taking actions that increase (known as expansionary policies) or decrease (known as contractionary policies) the total amount of money in circulation, the Fed has a major impact on total spending. It has various techniques at its disposal:

- **Reserve requirements**—The Fed sets requirements on banks as to the percentage of checking deposit money received from customers that may not be loaned out.

- **Open-market operations**—The Fed can buy or sell government securities on the open market and thereby increase or decrease the money supply outstanding.

- **Discount rate**—The Fed can change the cost of money to banks and thereby cause a change in interest rates throughout the economy.

Focus on

Economics, Strategy, and Globalization—Module 42

Unemployment

The unemployment rate is the percentage of those people who are looking for work who are currently not employed. There are three types of unemployment:

1. **Frictional**—This represents the time period during which people are unemployed as a result of changing jobs or newly entering the workforce. Because of the mobility of society, there is always some level of this type of unemployment, even in a society that effectively has "full" employment.

2. **Structural**—This represents potential workers whose job skills do not match the needs of the workforce as a result of changing demand for goods and services of technological advances that reduce or eliminate the need for the skills they possess. Such unemployment normally requires retraining in order for these individuals to be employable again.

3. **Cyclical**—This represents the unemployment caused by variations in the business cycle, when real GDP fails to grow at the pace necessary to employ all willing workers.

Focus on

Economics, Strategy, and Globalization—Module 42

Indicators of Business Cycles

Leading indicator—A measure that is being used to try to predict recoveries and recessions. These indicators will normally start moving up months before an actual recovery begins and start moving down months before an actual recession beings. There are many such indicators with variable success in predicting the business cycle. One of the most useful is changes in **stock market prices**.

Coincident indicator—A measure that normally moves up and down simultaneously with economic recoveries and recessions, respectively, and is used to determine if the economy is expanding or contracting at the present time. One example is **industrial production**.

Lagging indicator—A measure that normally starts moving up months after a recovery has begun and starts declining months after a recession has begun. It is used to confirm evidence that the economy has been expanding or contracting over the past few months. A commonly used lagging indicator is the **average prime rate** for bank loans.

Focus on

Economics, Strategy, and Globalization—Module 42

International Trade

Because of differences in resources, climate, and specific skills, countries that trade goods and services with each other normally raise the standard of living of the people in both nations. Each country will focus on its advantages:

- **Absolute advantage**—This exists when the country can produce the goods at a lower cost than the other country.

- **Comparative advantage**—This exists when the cost of producing those goods relative to the cost of producing other goods is lower in that country than in the other country.

Even if one country has an absolute advantage over the other with respect to all goods, there will be trade benefits to both from each focusing on its comparative advantage. (On an individual level, a skilled CPA who is able to type 80 words per minute would still benefit from having word processing performed by a secretary who can type only 40 words per minute and who has no accounting skills.)

Focus on

Economics, Strategy, and Globalization—Module 42

Obstacles to Free Trade

Free trade is restricted by **tariffs** (taxes on the importing of goods) and quotas (limits on the quantity that may be imported). When restrictions are imposed, their **direct** effects are:

- *Domestic producers: Positive.* Their demand curve shifts to the right as the availability of substitute goods has been reduced. They sell more goods at higher prices. Usually the managements and unions of these producers sought the restrictions.

- *Domestic users: Negative.* Their supply curve is being shifted to the left. As a result, they end up paying higher prices and acquiring fewer goods overall.

- *Foreign producers: Negative.* Their demand curve shifts to the left because the number of potential buyers has been reduced. They sell fewer goods at lower prices.

- *Foreign users: Positive.* Their supply curve shifts to the right, as their producers will have to do more selling in their own market. They buy more goods at lower prices.

A crucial **indirect** effect of trade restrictions is retaliation by other countries. The **World Trade Organization (WTO)** was formed to encourage all countries to maintain free trade policies and to prevent trade wars. The **North American Free Trade Agreement (NAFTA)** was signed by the United States, Mexico, and Canada in order to remove trade restrictions existing between those countries.

Balance of Payments

This is an account summary of the transactions of a nation with others.

Current account—The flow of goods and services and government transfers during a specific period of time:

- **Balance of trade**—The difference between the goods exported and good imported. If exports are higher, then a trade surplus exists; if imports are higher, a deficit exists.
- **Balance of goods and services**—The same comparison, but with services included

Capital account—The flow of investments in fixed and financial assets

Balance of payments—The combined surplus or deficit from the current and capital accounts

Official reserve account—The total of gold and foreign currency held by the nation

Focus on

Economics, Strategy, and Globalization—Module 42

Foreign Exchange Rates

The value of the currencies of different nations will fluctuate relative to one another based on the supply and demand for these currencies. Exchange rates between currencies include:

- **Spot rate**—The exchange rate for currencies that will be immediately delivered
- **Forward rate**—The rate at which two parties agree they will exchange the currencies at a specific future date (called the settlement date)

Forward rates differ from spot rates based on expectations that the relative values of the two currencies will change between now and then. Factors affecting foreign exchange rates:

- **Inflation**—The currency with higher inflation will fall in value relative to the other.
- **Interest rates**—The currency in the nation with higher interest rates will rise in value.
- **Balance of payments**—The currency of the country that is a net exporter will rise in value.
- **Government intervention**—The currency will rise if official reserves are used to buy it.
- **Political and economic stability**—The currency will fall when there are threats to stability.

Strategic Planning

Strategic planning involves identifying an organization's long-term goals and determining the best approaches to achieving those goals.

- Develop mission
- Develop vision
- Perform situational analysis to identify internal and external forces that may affect the organization's performance and choice of strategies and assess the organization's strengths, weaknesses, opportunities, and threats (a SWOT analysis)

Generic Strategies

- Product differentiation
- Cost leadership

Focus on

Economics, Strategy, and Globalization—Module 42

FINANCIAL RISK MANAGEMENT

Expected Returns

The total return of an investment includes cash distributions (interest, dividends, rents) and the change in the value of the asset. For example, an investment of $100 that pays a dividend of $3 and then grows in value to $107 at the end of the year has a total return of 10%.

Gordon equation: Total return = Current dividend rate + Annual rate of dividend increase

Expresses total return only in terms of future cash distributions by assuming increased value will allow future distributions. For example, 3% current dividend rate + 7% expected rate of dividend increase = 10%. The effect is identical to adding dividend and value growth.

A group of investments in similar types of assets is known as a **portfolio**. The expected return on a portfolio is a weighted average of the expected return of the individual investments.

For example, if a portfolio is invested 60% in Asset A, which is expected to return 10%, and 40% in Asset B, which is expected to return 5%, the expected portfolio return is 8%, as follows:

$$60\% \times 10\% + 40\% \times 5\% = 6\% + 2\% = 8\%$$

Average Returns

When measuring average returns, there are two different measures:

1. **Arithmetic average returns**—The result of adding different returns and dividing by the number of periods

2. **Geometric average returns**—The consistent return that would grow to the same final result as the actual returns of several different periods

For example, if an investment grew by 44% in one year and 0% in the next, then $100 would have grown to $144 in the first year and remained there in the second.

Arithmetic average return = 22% (the average of 44% and 0%)

Geometric average return = 20% (An investment of $100 earning a consistent 20% each year would grow to $120 after one year and $144 after two years.)

Focus on

Financial Risk Management and Capital Budgeting—Module 43

Standard Deviation

The most common measure of investment risk is **standard deviation (SD)**, which is a measure of the volatility of an investment. To calculate the SD, take the following steps:

1. Determine the arithmetic average return.
2. Calculate the difference from the average for each individual period.
3. Square the differences.
4. Determine the average of the squared values.
5. Calculate the square root of this average.

In general, since most investors are **risk averse**, an investment with a higher standard deviation (such as common stocks) would have a higher expected return, and an investment with a lower standard deviation (such as bonds) would have a lower expected return.

Focus on

Financial Risk Management and Capital Budgeting—Module 43

Standard Deviation (continued)

As an example, assume an investment has returned 7%, 15%, and 8% in three different periods.

1. (7% + 15% + 8%) / 3 = 10% arithmetic average return.
2. −3%, +5%, −2% are the differences from average in the three periods.
3. 9%, 25%, 4% are the squares of the differences.
4. (9% + 25% + 4%) / 3 = 12.67% average of the squared values.
5. SQR of 12.67% = 3.56%

Notice that the SD of 3.56% is slightly higher than the straight average of the differences:

$$(3\% + 5\% + 2\%) / 3 = 3.33\%$$

This is because the calculation of the SD gives disproportionate weight to bigger differences.

Portfolio Risk

The SD of a portfolio of investments will generally be much smaller than the SD of the individual investments, because different investments don't move up and down at the exact same time. The measure of the degree to which different investments move together is **covariance** or **correlation**.

Covariance = 1.00. When one investment goes up, the other always goes up. When one goes down, the other always goes down.

Covariance = 0. There is no relationship between the two investments; whether one goes up or down has no relationship to whether the other goes up or down.

Covariance = −1.00. When one investment goes up, the other always goes down. When one goes down, the other always goes up.

Whenever the covariance between two investments is less than 1.00, the SD of the portfolio will be lower than the average SD of the individual investments. This is because the differences in movement will somewhat offset each other.

By combining investments that have low covariances with each other, an investor can eliminate **unsystematic (unique) risk**. The unavoidable risk that remains is **systematic risk**.

Loan Risks

Creditors face certain business risks when they make loans:

- **Credit or default risk**—The risk that the borrower will default on interest or principal payments.
- **Sector risk**—The credit risk associated with conditions in the borrower's industry.
- **Concentration of credit risk**—The credit risk associated with lending to a small number of borrowers or borrowers with common sector risks. This is an unsystematic risk that can be eliminated through adequate diversification of loan portfolios.
- **Market risk**—The risk that the value of a bond or loan will decline due to a decline in the aggregate value of all the assets in the economy.
- **Interest rate risk**—The risk that the value of a bond or loan will decline due to an increase in interest rates.

Focus on

Financial Risk Management and Capital Budgeting—Module 43

Yield Curve

The interest rate charged on loans (and paid on bonds) varies based on the term of the loan. This is often charted with the x-axis (horizontal) being the term of the loan and the y-axis (vertical) being the interest rate. This chart is known as the **yield curve**:

- **Normal yield curve**—An upward-sloping curve with rates rising as time gets longer
- **Inverted yield curve**—A downward curve with rates on long-term loans being lower
- **Flat yield curve**—A curve with rates being about the same regardless of length

Theories on the reason for differences in yields include:

- **Liquidation preference**—Since long-term loans are less liquid and subject to more interest rate risk, they ought to normally offer higher yields.
- **Market segmentation**—Different lenders will dominate in different loan lengths: banks favor short-term loans, savings and loans favor intermediate-term loans, and life insurance companies favor long-term loans. Rates depend on the demands of lenders in those segments.
- **Expectations**—Long-term rates reflect expected changes in future short-term rates, with inflation expectations playing a major part in determining such rates.

Focus on

Financial Risk Management and Capital Budgeting—Module 43

Derivatives

A contract whose value derives from another contract or asset is a derivative if:

- **Settlement** of the contract will involve transfers of cash or other liquid assets.
- There is an **underlying** index that will be used to settle the contract **and** there is a specific **notional amount** (quantity) of that index to calculate the settlement.
- **No payment** is made at origination (other than an option premium, if applicable).

Specific types of derivatives include:

- **Option**—Contract allowing (but not requiring) the holder to buy (call) or sell (put) a commodity or financial instrument. The holder pays some premium to the other party.
- **Forward**—Negotiated contract to purchase and sell a commodity, financial instrument, or foreign currency at a future date at terms set at the origination of the contract.
- **Future**—Standardized forward-based contract trading on a public market.
- **Currency swap**—Forward-based contract to swap different currencies.
- **Interest rate swap**—Forward-based contract to swap interest payment agreements.

Risks Associated with Derivatives

Derivatives are used in two different ways:

1. **Speculation**—An investment intended to profit from price changes in the underlying
2. **Hedge**—An attempt to mitigate some business risk faced by the firm

Various business risks are associated with the use of derivatives:

- **Credit risk**—The risk that the counterparty to the contract will fail to honor its obligations.
- **Market risk**—The risk that the adverse changes will affect the fair value of the derivative. This risk is applicable only to derivatives used for speculation.
- **Legal risk**—The risk that legal or regulatory action will invalidate the derivative.
- **Basis risk**—The risk that the index used in connection with a derivative hedge will not fluctuate by the same amount as the contract or asset that is being hedged.

Using Derivatives as Hedges

There are three types of derivative hedges:

1. **Fair value hedge**—A hedge against a recognized asset or liability or a firm purchase or sale commitment.

2. **Cash flow hedge**—A hedge against possible variations in future expected cash flows.

3. **Foreign currency hedge**—A hedge against the effects of fluctuations in the value of a foreign currency. Most of these are forms of fair value or cash flow hedge.

Derivatives are always measured at fair value. Unrealized gains and losses are reported as follows:

- **Fair value hedge**—Changes in fair value are reported in earnings, offset by the changes in the asset, liability, or commitment being hedged. There will be a net effect on earnings only to the extent the hedge was ineffective.

- **Cash flow hedge**—Changes in fair value are reported in other comprehensive income to extent the hedge is effective with the remainder reported in earnings.

Focus on

Financial Risk Management and Capital Budgeting—Module 43

89

Valuing Derivatives

For derivatives that trade on public markets, determining fair value is straightforward. For others, pricing models may be needed.

Options may be valued using mathematical models such as:

- Black-Scholes model
- Monte Carlo simulation
- Binomial trees

Interest rate swaps are usually valued using the zero-coupon method.

The calculations used in these various models are generally complex and require specialized knowledge or access to computer programs.

Time Value of Money

Many decisions require adjustments related to the time value of money:

- **Present value of amount**—This is used to examine a single cash flow that will occur at a future date and determine its equivalent value today.

- **Present value of ordinary annuity**—This refers to repeated cash flows on a systematic basis, with amounts being paid at the end of each period. (It may also be known as an annuity in arrears.) Bond interest payments are commonly made at the end of each period and use these factors.

- **Present value of annuity due**—This refers to repeated cash flows on a systematic basis, with amounts being paid at the beginning of each period. (It may also be known as an annuity in advance or special annuity.) Rent payments are commonly made at the beginning of each period and use these factors.

- **Future values**—These look at cash flows and project them to some future date, and include all three variations applicable to present values.

- **Interest rates**—Usually, two components:
  1. Expected inflation/deflation rates
  2. Inflation-adjusted return for the investment (risk adjusted)

CAPITAL BUDGETING

Used to evaluate capital expenditures—uses two equations

    Cash inflows before tax

− Depreciation on investment

= Increase in taxable income

− Tax

= Increase in accounting net income

    Cash inflows before tax

− Tax

= After-tax net cash inflows

or

    Increase in accounting net income

+ Depreciation on investment

= After-tax net cash inflows

Payback Method

Initial investment

÷ After tax net cash inflows

= Payback period

Payback period is compared to target period

- If shorter, investment is acceptable
- If longer, investment is unacceptable

Traditional payback method does not take into account time value of money

Present value payback method considers the time value of money

Accounting Rate of Return

Increase in accounting net income

$\div$ Investment

$=$ Accounting rate of return

Investment may be

- Initial investment
- Long-term average – (Initial investment + Salvage value) / 2
- Short-term average – (Beginning carrying value + Ending carrying value) / 2

Return compared to target rate

- If greater, investment is acceptable
- If lower, investment is unacceptable

Accounting rate of return does not consider the time value of money

Internal Rate of Return

    Initial investment

÷   After tax net cash inflows

=   Present value factor (same as payback period)

Present value factor is compared to factors for same # of periods (life of investment) to determine effective interest rate

- Factor may be equal to amount at specific interest rate
- If factor falls between amounts, rate is estimated

Resulting rate compared to target rate

- If greater, investment is acceptable
- If lower, investment is unacceptable

Net Present Value

      After-tax net cash inflows

$\times$ Present value factor for annuity at target rate

$=$ Present value of investment

$-$ Initial investment

$=$ Net present value

If positive, investment is acceptable—if negative, investment is unacceptable

Focus on

Financial Risk Management and Capital Budgeting—Module 43

Special Analyses for Decision Making

Sensitivity analysis used to evaluate results of decisions under various conditions

Probability Analysis

Long-term average result (expected value) of decision is estimated

1. Each possible outcome of decision is assigned a probability
2. Total of probabilities is 100%
3. Profit or loss under each possible outcome is determined
4. Profit or loss for outcome multiplied by probability
5. Total of results is added
6. Result is long-term average result

Focus on

Financial Risk Management and Capital Budgeting—Module 43

Relevant Costing

Increase or decrease in profits or costs resulting from decision is analyzed

1. Determine increase or decrease in revenues that will result from decision
2. Determine increase or decrease in variable costs that will result from decision
3. Determine if decision will affect fixed costs
4. Net of change in revenues, variable costs, and fixed costs is relevant cost of making decision

Lease versus Buy: Compare Both Options Using Discounted Cash Flow

1. Leasing may require lower initial investment
2. Operating leases off balance sheet
3. Capital leases shift risk of ownership from lessor to lessee

Focus on

Financial Risk Management and Capital Budgeting—Module 43

FINANCIAL MANAGEMENT

Five functions:

1. **Financing**—Raising capital to fund the business
2. **Capital budgeting**—Selecting the best long-term projects based on risk and return
3. **Financial management**—Managing cash flow so that funds are available when needed at the lowest cost
4. **Corporate governance**—Ensuring behavior by managers that is ethical and in the best interests of shareholders
5. **Risk management**—Identifying and managing the firm's exposure to all types of risk

Focus on

Financial Management—Module 44

Working Capital Management

Inventory conversion period (ICP)—The average number of days required to convert inventory to sales

- ICP = Average inventory / Cost of sales per day
- Average inventory = (Beginning inventory + Ending inventory) / 2
- Assume 365 days in a year unless told otherwise

Receivables collection period (RCP)—The average number of days required to collect accounts receivable

- RCP = Average receivables / Credit sales per day

Payables deferral period (PDP)—The average number of days between the purchase of inventory (including materials and labor for a manufacturing entity) and payment for them

- PDP = Average payables / Purchases per day

Cash conversion cycle (CCC)—The average number of days between the payment of cash to suppliers of material and labor and cash inflows from customers

- CCC = ICP + RCP – PDP

Cash Management

Cash balances are maintained by a firm for:

- **Operations**—To pay ordinary expenses
- **Compensating balances**—To receive various bank services, fee waivers, and loans
- **Trade discounts**—Quick payment of bills for early payment discounts
- **Speculative balances**—Funds to take advantage of special business opportunities
- **Precautionary balances**—Amounts that may be needed in emergency situations

Float refers to the time it takes for checks to be mailed, processed, and reflected in accounts. Management techniques try to maximize float on payments and minimize it on receipts.

- **Zero-balance accounts**—The firm is notified each day of checks presented for payment and transfers only the funds needed to cover them.
- **Lockbox system**—Customers send payments directly to bank to speed up deposits.
- **Concentration banking**—Customers pay to local branches instead of main offices.
- **Electronic funds transfers**—Customers pay electronically for fastest processing.

Focus on

Financial Management—Module 44

Marketable Securities

To maximize earnings on free cash, a firm may utilize various investments. Investments that are available through the federal government include:

- **Treasury bills**—Short-term obligations backed by the United States with original lives under 1 year that can be bought and sold easily from issuance to maturity date. These are in zero-coupon form and pay no formal interest, so they trade at a discount to maturity value.

- **Treasury notes**—Obligations with initial lives between 1 to 10 years. Formal interest payments are made semiannually.

- **Treasury bonds**—Same as notes but with original lives over 10 years.

- **Treasury Inflation-Protected Securities (TIPS)**—Treasury notes and bonds that pay a fixed rate of interest but with principal adjusted semiannually for inflation.

- **Federal agency securities**—Offerings that may or may not be backed by the full faith and credit of the United States and don't trade as actively as Treasuries but pay slightly higher rates.

Marketable Securities (continued)

Other possible investments with free cash include:

- **Certificates of deposit**—Time deposits at banks that have limited government insurance.

- **Commercial paper**—Promissory notes from corporations with lives up to 9 months.

- **Banker's acceptance**—A draft drawn on a bank but payable at a specific future date (not on demand, as checks would be), usually 30 to 90 days after being drawn. These are usually generated by corporations to pay for goods, and may trade in secondary markets prior to the due date for payment at a discount.

- **Money market fund**—Shares in a mutual fund that invests in instruments with an average maturity date under 90 days, and which generally maintains a stable value for investors.

- **Short-term bond fund**—Shares in a mutual fund that invests in instruments with an average life over 90 days but under 5 years, generating higher returns than a money market fund but with some fluctuation in the principal value of the fund.

- **Equity and debt securities**—Individual stocks and bonds with substantially higher potential returns but also greater risk, including the risk of default. Should consider purchasing credit default insurance.

Focus on

Financial Management—Module 44

Inventory Management

Economic Order Quantity (EOQ)

Minimizes total of order cost and carrying cost:

- **Order cost**—Cost of placing an order or starting a production run
- **Carrying cost**—Cost of having inventory on hand

$$EOQ = \sqrt{2AP/S}$$

A = Annual demand in units

P = Cost of placing an order or beginning a production run

S = Cost of carrying one unit in inventory for one period

Focus on

Financial Management—Module 44

Reorder Point and Safety Stock

Reorder point

- Units in inventory when order should be placed
- Average daily demand × Average lead time = Reorder point

Safety stock

- Extra units in inventory when placing order in case demand or lead time is greater than average
- Avoids costs associated with running out of stock
- Maximum daily demand × Maximum lead time − Reorder point = Safety stock

Just-in-Time (JIT) Purchasing

Costs reduced through:

- Reduction in inventory quantities
- Elimination of non-value-adding operations
- Most appropriate when order cost low and carrying cost high

Requires high-quality control standards

- Efficient system minimizing defective units
- Corrections made as defects occur
- Fewer vendors and suppliers

Just-in-Time (JIT) Purchasing (continued)

Problems of JIT system:

- Difficult to find suppliers able to accommodate
- High shipping costs due to smaller orders
- Potential problems due to delays in deliveries

May use backflush approach

- All manufacturing costs charged to cost of goods sold (COGS)
- Costs allocated from COGS to inventories at reporting dates

Receivables Management

A company sets credit policies for the granting and monitoring of receivables, including:

- **Credit period**—The time allowed for payment (typically 30 days)
- **Discounts**—Percentage reduction for early payment (such as 2% for payment in 10 days)
- **Credit criteria**—Financial strength requirements for customer to be granted credit
- **Collection policy**—Methods used to collect slow-paying accounts

In utilizing receivables to generate immediate cash, a firm's receivables may be:

- **Pledged**—A loan is obtained with the receivables offered as collateral for the loan.
- **Factored**—The receivables are actually sold to a financing company, which accepts the risk of noncollection and charges a percentage fee for accepting that risk (based on an estimate of the uncollectibles rate) as well as an interest rate based on the funds advanced prior to the date collection of the receivables is due.

Capital Structure

Long-Term Debt

Private debt—Loans obtained from banks and other financial institutions or from syndicates of lenders. Virtually all such loans have variable interest rates that are tied to an index:

- **Prime rate**—This is the rate that the lender charges its most creditworthy customers. Loans to other customers would include a fixed amount above this (e.g., prime plus 2%).

- **London Interbank Offered Rate (LIBOR)**—When the borrower and lender are in different countries, the base used will typically be the LIBOR rather than the prime rate.

Public debt—To bypass institutional lenders, a corporation may sell bonds directly to investors as a means of borrowing, with fixed interest rates and maturity dates for the securities, which can then trade on the open market.

- **SEC registered bonds**—To be sold on U.S. markets, bonds must satisfy the stringent registration and disclosure requirements of the SEC.

- **Eurobonds**—Bonds denominated in U.S. dollars can be sold on the European exchanges, which have less stringent requirements.

Debt Covenants

Borrowers often must agree to obey restrictions, or debt covenants.

Positive covenants might include:

- Providing annual audited financial statements to the lender
- Maintaining minimum ratios of current assets to current liabilities or financial measures
- Maintaining life insurance policies on key officers or employees of the company

Negative covenants might include:

- Not borrowing additional sums during the time period from other lenders
- Not selling certain assets of the business
- Not paying dividends to shareholders
- Not exceeding certain compensation limits for executives

Secured and Unsecured Bonds

Debt obligations may be secured by certain collateral or may specifically be placed behind other forms of debt in the priority of repayment. In roughly declining order of safety (and increasing order of interest rate), there are:

- **Mortgage bonds**—Secured by certain real estate owned by the borrower
- **Collateral trust bonds**—Secured by financial assets of the firm
- **Debentures**—Unsecured bonds
- **Subordinated debentures**—Unsecured bonds that will be repaid after all other creditors in the event of a liquidation of the corporation
- **Income bonds**—Bonds whose interest payments will be made only out of earnings of the corporation

Focus on

Financial Management—Module 44

Provisions Affecting Repayment of Bonds

The repayment of bonds may be affected by various provisions:

- **Term bonds**—Principal will be repaid on a single maturity date.
- **Serial bonds**—Principal repayment will occur in installments.
- **Sinking funds**—Regular deposits will be made by the borrower into an account from which repayment of the bonds will be made.

- **Convertible bonds**—The bondholder may convert the bonds to the common stock of the company as a form of repayment instead of holding them to maturity for cash.

- **Redeemable bonds**—The bondholder may be able to demand repayment of the bonds in advance of the normal maturity date should certain events occur (such as the buyout of the company by another firm).

- **Callable bonds**—The borrowing firm may force the bondholders to redeem the bonds before their normal maturity date (usually there is a set premium above the normal redemption price to compensate them for this forced liquidation).

Bond Interest Rates

There are three interest rates relevant to bonds:

1. **Stated rate**—The fixed interest payment calculated from the face value of the bond. It is also known as the **coupon rate, face rate,** or **nominal rate.**

2. **Current yield**—The fixed interest payment divided by the current selling price of the bond. When the bond is trading at a discount, this rate will be higher than the stated rate, and when the bond is trading at a premium, this rate will be lower than the stated rate. This rate can be somewhat misleading, since it reports the interest payment as a percentage of the current price but doesn't take into account the fact that the principal repayment of the bond will not be the current selling price but the face value.

3. **Yield to maturity**—The interest rate at which the present value of the cash flows of interest and principal will equal the current selling price of the bonds. For a bond selling at a discount, it will be even higher than the current yield, since it accounts for the "bonus" interest payment reflected in the discount. For a bond selling at a premium, this rate will be even lower than the current yield, since it reflects the loss of the premium when the principal is repaid. This rate is also known as the **effective rate** or **market rate.**

Variations on Bond Interest

Zero-coupon bond—This bond makes no interest payments at all and only pays the face value on the date of maturity. Short-term U.S. Treasury bills are a common example. A zero-coupon bond will always sell at a discount, since the interest is represented entirely by the difference between the price at which it is bought and the face value paid at maturity.

Floating rate bond—The interest payment is not fixed but fluctuates with some general index of interest rates. A **reverse floater** actually pays more interest when the general index goes down and less interest when the index goes up. Such an unusual bond might be used to hedge against the risk associated with floating rate bonds that the firm has issued.

Registered bond—The bondholder's name is registered with the firm, and interest payments are sent directly to the registered owner. In such cases, an actual bond certificate usually will not be issued.

Junk bond—This bond pays much higher than normal interest, since it was issued by a firm that has a poor credit rating and is more likely to default on its obligations. Bonds with a credit rating by Moody's Investors Service lower than Baa are usually considered junk bonds.

Foreign bond—This simply refers to a bond in which interest and principal is paid in another currency.

Common Stock

Common stock shareholders are entitled to the residual (or leftover) assets and income after all creditors and preferred shareholders are paid.

Advantages to firm:

- The firm has no specific obligation to pay investors, increasing financial flexibility.
- Increased equity reduces the risk to lenders and reduces borrowing costs.

Disadvantages to firm:

- Issuance costs are greater than for debt.
- Ownership and control must be shared with all the new shareholders.
- Dividends are not tax-deductible.
- Shareholders ultimately receive a much higher return than lenders if the business is successful, so the long-run cost of capital obtained this way is typically much higher.

Preferred Stock

Preferred stock shareholders receive a stipulated dividend and priority over common shareholders in the event of liquidation of the business. Additional features preferred stock may include:

- **Cumulative dividends**—If stipulated dividends are not declared in a particular year, the amount becomes dividends in arrears and must be paid in later years before the common shareholders can receive any distribution.

- **Redeemability**—The shareholders may demand repayment of the face value at a specific date. In some cases, redemption is automatic. Such shares more closely resemble debt and are often presented before equity in the balance sheet.

- **Callability**—The firm may force the shareholders to redeem the shares.

- **Convertibility**—Shareholders can convert these shares to common stock.

- **Participation**—Preferred shareholders will receive a dividend that is higher than the stipulated rate when the common shareholders receive a higher rate.

- **Floating rate**—The dividend is variable based on some interest or inflation index.

Leverage

Operating leverage—The degree to which a firm has built fixed costs into its operations

- Higher fixed costs mean more risk when revenues are below expectations
- Profit grows rapidly relative to revenue increases due to lower variable costs
- % change in operating income / % change in unit volume = Degree of operating leverage

Financial leverage—The degree to which a firm uses debt financing in its business

- Higher debt means higher interest and principal obligations for repayment, increasing risk if performance is not up to expectations
- Debt financing costs less than equity financing and doesn't increase with greater performance, so overall profit and asset growth potential is greater
- % change in earnings per share / % change in earnings before interest and taxes = Degree of financial leverage

Cost of Capital

Debt—The cost of debt financing is the after-tax cost of interest payments, as measured by the yield to maturity. It can be calculated in two ways:

1. Yield to maturity $\times$ (1 − Effective tax rate)
2. (Interest expense − Tax deduction for interest) / Carrying value of debt

Preferred stock—The cost of preferred stock financing is the stipulated dividend divided by the issue price of the stock.

Common stock—The cost of common stock financing represents the expected returns of the common shareholders and is difficult to estimate. Some techniques:

- **Capital asset pricing model (CAPM)**—Volatility of stock price relative to average stock. This model assumes the expected return of a particular stock depends on its volatility (beta) relative to the overall stock market. CAPM = Beta × Excess of normal market return over risk-free investments + Normal return on risk-free investments

- **Arbitrage pricing model**—This model is a more sophisticated CAPM with separate excess returns and betas for each component making up the stock characteristics

Cost of Capital (continued)

- **Bond yield plus**—This uses the normal historical relationship between equities and debt and simply adds 3% to 5% to the interest rate on the firm's long-term debt

- **Dividend yield plus growth rate**—This takes the current dividend as a percentage of the stock price and adds the expected growth rate in earnings

Weighted-average cost of capital—This is a calculation of a firm's effective cost of capital, taking into account the portion of its capital that was obtained by debt, preferred stock, and common stock. For example, if 40% of capital was obtained through long-term debt at an effective cost of 6%, 10% of capital was obtained by issuing preferred stock with an effective cost of 8%, and 50% of capital was obtained by issuing common stock expected to return 11% to shareholders, the weighted-average cost of capital is:

$$40\% \times 6\% + 10\% \times 8\% + 50\% \times 11\%$$

$$= 2.4\% + 0.8\% + 5.5\%$$

$$= 8.7\%$$

Mergers

Horizontal merger—When a firm acquires another in the same line of business (a competitor)

Vertical merger—When a firm acquires another in the same supply chain (a supplier or customer)

Conglomerate merger—When a firm acquires another in an unrelated line of business

In valuing a potential merger target, the company may use:

- **Discounted cash flow analysis**—The present value of the cash flows expected from the acquisition of the company, discounted at the cost of equity capital

- **Market multiple method**—The current earnings of the company multiplied by the price-earnings ratio that is appropriate to that company (based on factors such as the typical ratio in that industry)

Asset and Liability Valuation

Three major valuation models for financial instruments assets in order of reliability:

1. Market values from active markets for identical assets
   a. Assumes sufficient volume
2. Active markets for similar assets
   a. Must adjust for differences in instruments, for example,
      1) Block sales
      2) Credit risks
      3) Maturity/exercise dates
3. Valuation models
   a. In absence of active markets, assume hypothetical seller/buyer
   b. Generally use discounted cash flow
   c. Must use assumptions that are reasonable and consistent with existing general market information

PERFORMANCE MEASURES AND MANAGEMENT TECHNIQUES

Measurement Frameworks

Balanced scorecards attempt to translate an organization's goals into specific measures with four perspectives:

1. **Financial**—Return on investment and related financial measures
2. **Customer**—Nonfinancial measures of customer satisfaction and retention
3. **Internal business processes**—Measures of operating effectiveness and efficiency including financial measures, such as cost variances, and nonfinancial measures, such as number of defects in production
4. **Learning and growth**—Measures of employee satisfaction, training, and advancement

Value-based management examines all aspects of a company with the intention of identifying the amount of **economic value added (EVA)** by different activities. In effect, it attempts to translate all activities into their financial value to the firm, and is comparable to a financial scorecard focus.

Balanced Scorecard

The components of a balanced scorecard include:

- **Strategic objectives**—A statement of the goals of the firm and necessary elements
- **Performance measures**—Identification of quantitative methods that can be used to track success in fulfilling the strategic objectives
- **Baseline performance**—The current level of performance for each measure
- **Targets**—The level or improvement in performance being sought
- **Strategic initiatives**—Programs that will help achieve the targets and objectives

Cause-and-effect linkages identify which performance measures are **performance drivers** (leading indicators) and which are **outcome performance measures** (lagging indicators). This allows the firm to focus on those drivers that are critical to strategic objectives.

Strategy maps are diagrams that identify cause-and-effect linkages:

Focus on

Value-Based Management

Return on Investment (based on assets) = Net income / Total assets

DuPont return on investment (ROI) analysis: ROI = Return on sales × Asset turnover

- **Return on sales** = Net income / Sales
- **Asset turnover** = Sales / Total assets

Residual income = Operating profit − Interest on investment

- **Interest on investment** = Invested capital × Required rate of return

Economic Value Added: EVA = Net operating profit after taxes (NOPAT) − Cost of financing

- **Cost of financing** = (Total assets − Current liabilities) × Weighted-average cost of capital

Free Cash Flow = NOPAT + Depreciation + Amortization − Capital expenditures − Net increase in working capital

Focus on

Performance Measures and Management Techniques—Module 45

Business Process Management: Focus on Continuous Improvement in Processes to Meet Customers' Needs

Business Processes: Assets in Themselves

1. Design: Identify existing processes/possible improvements
2. Modeling: What-if analyses
3. Execution
   a. Install new software
   b. Test
   c. Train employees
   d. Implement new processes
4. Monitor with performance statistics
5. Optimize
   a. Use performance statistics to identify bottlenecks
   b. Consider strategies (e.g., outsourcing) to remove bottlenecks

Focus on

Performance Measures and Management Techniques—Module 45

Business Process Management: Focus on Continuous Improvement in Processes to Meet Customers' Needs (continued)

6. Other techniques

   a. Reengineer

   b. Lean manufacturing (shorten time by eliminating waste)

   c. Theory of constraints: Increase throughput contribution margin by decreasing investment and operating costs. Must identify and remediate:

      1) Bottleneck resources: capacity is less than demand

      2) Non-bottleneck resources: capacity greater than demand

7. Workflow analysis: Focus on eliminating non-value-added activities

Profitability Ratios

Gross Margin = Gross profit / Net sales

Operating Profit Margin = Operating profit / Net sales

Return on Assets = Net income / Average total assets

- **Average total assets** = (Beginning total assets + Ending total assets) / 2

Return on Equity = Net income / Average common stockholders' equity

- **Common stockholders' equity** = Stockholders' equity – Preferred stock liquidation value

Asset Utilization Ratios

Receivable Turnover = Net credit sales / Average accounts receivable

- **Average accounts receivable (A/R)** = (Beginning A/R + Ending A/R) / 2
- Remember to use net credit sales, **not** net sales

Receivables Collection Period = Average accounts receivable / Average credit sales per day

- Use 365-day year unless told otherwise

Inventory Turnover = Cost of goods sold / Average inventory

- Remember to use cost of goods sold, **not** sales

Inventory Conversion Period = Average inventory / Average cost of goods sold per day

Fixed Asset Turnover = Sales / Average net fixed assets

- Remember that net fixed assets is after subtraction of accumulated depreciation

Total Asset Turnover = Sales / Average total assets

Liquidity Ratios

Current Ratio = Current assets / Current liabilities

Quick (or Acid Test) Ratio = Quick assets / Current liabilities

- **Quick assets** = Cash + Marketable securities + Accounts receivable

Debt Utilization Ratios

Debt to Total Assets = Total liabilities / Total assets

Debt to Equity Ratio = Total debt / Total equity

Times Interest Earned Ratio = Earnings before interest and taxes / Interest expense

Focus on

Performance Measures and Management Techniques—Module 45

Market Ratios

Price/Earnings (PE) Ratio = Common stock price per share / Earnings per share

Book Value per Share = Common stock equity / Common stock shares outstanding

- **Common stock equity** = Stockholders' equity – Preferred stock liquidation value

Market Capitalization = Common stock price per share × Common stock shares outstanding

Market/Book Ratio can be calculated in two ways:

1. Common stock price per share / Book value per share
2. Market capitalization / Common stock equity

Benchmarking

Measures of performance need to be compared with expected or desired results. In selecting an approach **benchmark**, the firm may utilize any or all of the following:

- **Internal benchmarking**—Similar operations within the organization
- **Competitive benchmarking**—Direct competitors
- **Functional benchmarking**—Industry averages
- **Generic benchmarking**—Overall averages of all business enterprise

Benchmarks may represent average performance results or optimal results **(best practices)**.

Focus on

Performance Measures and Management Techniques—Module 45

Quality Control

ISO Quality Standards—A series of standards established by the International Organization of Standards.

- **ISO 9000 Series**—Standards consisting of five parts (9000 to 9004) that focus on the quality of products and services provided by firms

- **ISO 14000 Series**—Standards focused on pollution reduction and other environmental goals

Pareto Principle—An attempt to focus on the small number of significant quality issues, based on an estimate that 80% of all problems come from only 20% of all causes.

Six Sigma Quality—A statistical measure of the percentage of products that are in acceptable form, based on standard deviation measures. One sigma means that approximately 68% of products are acceptable. Six sigmas would indicate 99.999997% of products meet quality standards, and constitute a hypothetical goal of perfection in manufacturing.

Kaizen—Japanese art of continuous improvement. This theory emphasizes identification by all members of a company of small potential improvements rather than searching for big breakthroughs.

Delphi—Separate consultation with multiple experts and tabulation of recommendations.

Focus on

Performance Measures and Management Techniques—Module 45

Cost of Quality

The costs related to quality rise the later in the process the firm deals with it. There are four different stages at which costs can be addressed:

1. **Prevention costs**—Prevent product failure

   - Use high-quality materials
   - Inspect production process
   - Train employees
   - Maintain machines

2. **Appraisal or detection costs**—Detect product failure before production is complete

   - Inspect samples of finished goods
   - Obtain information from customers

Focus on

Performance Measures and Management Techniques—Module 45

Cost of Quality (continued)

3. **Internal failure costs**—Detect product failure after production but before shipment to customer

   - Scrap resulting from wasted materials
   - Reworking units to correct defects
   - Reinspection and retesting after rework

4. **External failure costs**—Defective product sent to customer

   - Warranty costs
   - Dealing with customer complaints
   - Product liability
   - Marketing to improve image
   - Lost sales

Project Management

A project is a series of activities and tasks that

- Have specific definable objectives
- Have defined start and end dates
- Are subject to funding constraints
- Consume resources, people, equipment, etc.
- Cut across various functional areas of the organization

Effective project management: Four basic elements

1. Resources
2. Time
3. Money
4. Scope

Project Management (continued)

Effective project management: Five processes/cycles

1. Project initiation
   a. Support of management
   b. Project manager with authority
   c. Project charter
2. Project planning
   a. Define scope
   b. Identify resources needed
   c. Schedule tasks
   d. Identify risks

Project Management (continued)

3. Project execution
   a. Managing work
   b. Directing team
4. Project monitoring and control
   a. Tracking progress
   b. Comparing actual outcomes to predicted outcomes (variances)
5. Project closure

Project Management Tools

1. Life-cycle approach: Define and assess each phase of project
2. Gantt chart—bar chart that illustrates the scheduled start and finish of elements of a project over time

Project Management (continued)

3. Program Evaluation and Review Technique (PERT): Focus on the interdependency of activities and the time required to complete an activity to schedule and control the project

 a. Critical path: The shortest amount of time necessary to accomplish the project.

   1) Optimistic
   2) Most likely
   3) Pessimistic

4. PERT used where there is a high variability of completion time, such as R&D

5. ABC analysis: Categorize tasks into three groups:

 a. Tasks that are perceived as being urgent and important
 b. Tasks that are important but not urgent
 c. Tasks that are neither urgent nor important

COST MEASUREMENT AND ASSIGNMENT

Cost Classifications

Product and Period Costs

	Product	Period
Direct materials (DM)	x	
Direct labor (DL)	x	
Manufacturing overhead (MOH)	x	
Selling, general, and administrative expenses (SG&A)		x

Prime and Conversion Costs

	Prime	Conversion
DM	x	
DL	x	x
MOH		x

Focus on

Cost Measurement and Assignment—Module 46

Cost Classifications (continued)

Variable and Fixed Costs

	Variable	Fixed
DM	x	
DL	x	
MOH	x	x
SG&A	x	x

Costing Methods

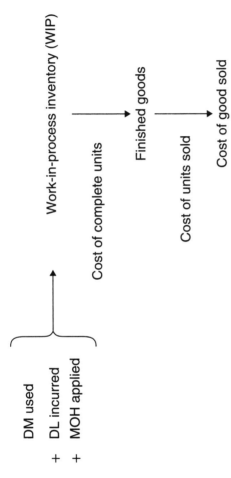

DM used
+ DL incurred
+ MOH applied

→ Work-in-process inventory (WIP)

Cost of complete units

→ Finished goods

Cost of units sold

→ Cost of good sold

Manufacturing Overhead

1. Calculate the predetermined overhead rate (POHR)

   Estimated variable MOH for period

   + Estimated fixed MOH for period

   = Estimated total MOH for period

   ÷ Estimated # of units for period (cost driver)

   = Predetermined overhead rate (POHR)—often split into fixed and variable rates

2. Apply MOH to WIP

   Actual # of units for period (cost driver)

   × POHR

   = MOH Applied

Manufacturing Overhead (continued)

3. Determine under-applied or over-applied MOH

    • Actual MOH > MOH applied: MOH under-applied

    • Actual MOH < MOH applied: MOH over-applied

4. Dispose of under-applied or over-applied MOH

    • Generally added to or deducted from cost of good sold (COGS)

    • May be charged or credited directly to income

    • May be allocated to WIP, finished goods, and COGS

Job Order Costing

Used when units are relatively expensive and costs can be identified to units or batches

- DM, DL, and MOH applied charged to WIP
- Cost of completed units removed from WIP and charged to finished goods
- Cost of units sold removed from finished goods and charged to COGS

Process Costing

Used when units are relatively inexpensive and costs cannot be identified to units or batches

- DM, DL, and MOH applied charged to WIP
- Calculates average cost of equivalent units produced during period
- Average costs used to transfer from WIP to finished goods and from finished goods to COGS

Calculating equivalent units

- Costs incurred at beginning of process—Equivalent units = Units × 100%
- Costs incurred at end of process—Equivalent units = Units × 0%
- Costs incurred uniformly—Equivalent units = Units × % complete
- Costs incurred at particular point
  - If units reached that point—Equivalent units = Units × 100%
  - If units haven't reached that point—Equivalent units = Units × 0%

Focus on

Cost Measurement and Assignment—Module 46

Process Costing (continued)

Process costing—weighted-average

1.
   Costs in beginning WIP
   + Costs incurred during period
   = Total costs to be allocated

2.
   Units completed during period
   + Equivalent units in ending WIP
   = Total equivalent production

3.
   Total costs to be allocated
   ÷ Total equivalent production
   = Average cost per equivalent unit

4.
   Units completed during period
   × Average cost per equivalent unit
   = Amount allocated to finished goods

5.
   Equivalent units in ending inventory
   × Average cost per equivalent unit
   = Amount allocated to ending WIP

Process Costing (continued)

Process costing—FIFO

1. Determine costs incurred during period

2. Units in beginning WIP

  − Equivalent units in beginning WIP

  = Equivalent units required to complete beginning WIP

3. Equivalent units required to complete beginning WIP

  ÷ Units started and completed during period × 100%

  + Equivalent units in ending WIP

  = Total equivalent production

Process Costing (continued)

4.   Costs incurred during period

    $\div$ Total equivalent production

    $=$ Average cost per equivalent unit

5.   Costs in beginning WIP

    $+$ Units started and completed $\times$ Average cost per equivalent unit

    $=$ Amount allocated to finished goods

6.   Equivalent units in ending WIP

    $\times$ Average cost per equivalent unit

    $=$ Amount allocated to ending WIP

Spoilage and Scrap

Different types of unused units or materials have different accounting treatments:

Normal spoilage—Product cost (added to cost of good units)

Abnormal spoilage—Period cost (charged against income in period)

Scrap—Generally charged to cost of goods manufactured

Proceeds from sale of scrap:

- Additional income
- Reduce cost of sales
- Reduce manufacturing overhead
- Reduce cost of specific job

Activity Based Costing (ABC)

Method of analyzing and reducing MOH

- MOH segregated into pools
- Cost driver identified for each pool
- MOH applied using multiple rates

Identifies costs that are nonvalue adding

- Can be used to reduce overhead
- Identify and minimize nonvalue adding costs

Also used to allocate service department costs

Under step allocation method

- Services departments allocated beginning with those serving most other departments
- Allocation based on that department's cost driver
- Costs allocated to all remaining service departments and production departments
- Costs not charged back to service departments already allocated
- Process complete when only production departments remain

Activity Based Costing (ABC) (continued)

		Service departments				Production departments	
		#1	**#2**	**#3**	**#4**	**#1**	**#2**
Costs		$	$	$	$	$	$
	Allocation	($)	$	$	$	$	$
Subtotal		0	$	$	$	$	$
	Allocation		($)	$	$	$	$
Subtotal			0	$	$	$	$
	Allocation			($)	$	$	$
Subtotal				0	$	$	$
	Allocation				($)	$	$
Total					0	$	$

Cost Estimation

Calculating Total Costs

Total costs = Fixed costs + Variable costs

$y = a + bx$

y = Total cost (dependent variable)

a = Total fixed costs

b = Variable cost per unit

x = # of units (independent variable)

Various methods are used to determine the variable cost per unit and total fixed costs

Cost Drivers

Units represent volume of cost driver

- Cost driver can be any variable that has greatest influence on cost
- Examples include volume of production, hours worked, miles driven, or machine hours

High-Low Method

Four steps in estimating variable cost per unit and total fixed costs

1. Highest volume   Total cost   # of units
   Lowest volume   Total cost   # of units
   Difference   Cost   # of units

2. Variable cost per unit = Difference in cost ÷ Difference in # of units
3. Total variable costs (at either level) = Variable cost per unit × # of units
4. Fixed costs (at either level) = Total costs − Total variable costs

Regression Analysis

Coefficient of correlation (R) indicates relationship between dependent and independent variable:

- R = 1   Strong direct relationship
- 1 > R > 0   Direct relationship, not as strong
- R = 0   No relationship
- 0 > R > −1   Indirect relationship, not as strong
- R = −1   Strong indirect relationship

Company will use cost driver with strongest direct or indirect relationship

Variable and Absorption Costing

Absorption Costing

- Used for financial statements
- Inventory includes DM + DL + Variable MOH + Fixed MOH

Variable Costing

- Used for internal purposes only
- Inventory includes DM + DL + Variable MOH

Absorption costing

    Sales
- Cost of sales
= Gross profit
- SG&A expenses
= Operation income

Variable costing

    Sales
- Variable costs
= Contribution margin
- Fixed costs
= Operation income

Difference = Change in inventory × Fixed overhead per unit

Focus on

Cost Measurement and Assignment—Module 46

PLANNING, CONTROL, AND ANALYSIS

Flexible Budgeting

Used to estimate revenue, costs, a group of costs, or profits at various levels of activity

- Applies when operating within a relevant range
- Total fixed costs remain the same at all levels within range
- Variable costs per unit of activity remains the same within range

Master and Static Budgets

Static budget—Budget as specific level of activity

- Can be for division of company
- Can be for company as a whole

Master budget—Static budget for company as a whole

Master budget generally includes:

- Operating budget
- Budgeted cash flows
- Budgeted financial statements

Preparing a Master Budget

1. Estimate sales volume

2. Use sales volume to estimate revenues

3. Use collection history to estimate collections

4. Estimate cost of sales based on units sold

5. Use current finished goods inventory, budgeted ending inventory, and cost of sales to estimate units to be manufactured

6. Use units manufactured to estimate material needs, labor costs, and overhead costs

7. Use material needs, current raw materials inventory, and budgeted ending inventory to budget purchases

8. Use purchase terms to estimate payments

9. Analyze expense and payment patterns to complete operating and cash flow budgets

Budgeting Material Purchases and Payments

Units sold

\+ Budgeted increase in finished goods

\- Budgeted decrease in finished goods

\= Units to be manufactured

× Units of raw material per unit of finished goods

\= Units of raw material required for production

\+ Budgeted increase in raw materials

\- Budgeted decrease in raw materials

\= **Budgeted raw material purchases**

\+ Budgeted decrease in accounts payable

\- Budgeted increase in accounts payable

\= **Budgeted payments for raw materials**

Focus on

Planning, Control, and Analysis—Module 47

Standard Costing

Material Variances

Standard cost (Units produced × Std qty per unit × Std cost per unit)
  − Actual material cost
  = Total material variance

      Material price variance (MPV)
  + Material usage variance (MUV)
  = Total material variance

MPV = Act qty × (Std pr − Act pr)   MUV = Std pr × (Std qty − Act qty)

Standard Costing (continued)

Labor Variances

Standard cost (Units produced × Std hrs per unit × Std rate per hr)

   − Actual labor cost

   = Total labor variance

        Labor rate variance (LRV)

    + Labor efficiency variance (LEV)

    = Total labor variance

LRV = Act qty × (Std rate − Act rate)   LEV = Std rate × (Std hrs − Act hrs)

Focus on

Planning, Control, and Analysis—Module 47

Standard Costing (continued)

Overhead Variances

Overhead applied (Std hrs × Total POHR)
- Actual overhead cost
= Total overhead variance

Overhead volume variance (OVV)
+ Overhead efficiency variance (OEV)
+ Overhead spending variance (OSV)
= Total overhead variance

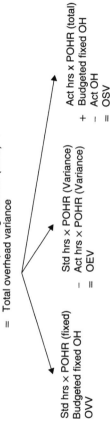

Std hrs × POHR (fixed)
- Budgeted fixed OH
= OVV

Std hrs × POHR (Variance)
- Act hrs × POHR (Variance)
= OEV

Act hrs × POHR (total)
Budgeted fixed OH
+ Act OH
- OSV
= OSV

Responsibility Accounting and Performance Evaluation

Company divisions may be:

- **Cost centers**—manager responsible for costs incurred
- **Profit centers**—manager responsible for costs and revenues
- **Investment centers**—manager responsible for costs, revenues, and capital investments

Focus on

Planning, Control, and Analysis—Module 47

Transfer Pricing

Transfer price—price at which products are transferred from one department to another within the same company

Possible transfer prices:

- Actual cost
- Market value
- Cost + profit
- Negotiated amount
- Standard cost

Transfer from cost center to profit center—generally use standard variable cost

- Cost center evaluated based on comparing standard variable cost to actual cost
- Profit center not affected by performance of cost center

Cost-Volume-Profit Analysis

Sales price per unit
− Variable cost per unit
= Contrib margin per unit

Units

Breakeven

Fixed costs
÷ Contrib margin per unit
= Breakeven in units

Profit as fixed amount

Fixed costs + Desired profit
÷ Contrib margin per unit
= Units required to earn desired profit

Profit as percentage of sales

Fixed costs
÷ Contrib margin − Profit per unit
= Units required to earn profit ratio

Contrib margin per unit
÷ Sales price per unit
= Contrib margin ratio

Dollars

Fixed costs
÷ Contrib margin ratio
= Breakeven in dollars

Fixed costs + Desired profit
÷ Contrib margin ratio
= Sales dollars required to earn desired profit

Fixed costs
÷ (Contrib margin − Profit) ÷ Sales price
= Sales required to earn profit ratio

Focus on

Planning, Control, and Analysis—Module 47

Graphical Approach to Breakeven

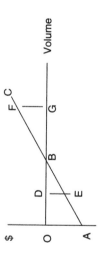

AC	= Profit for product at various levels of production
B	= Breakeven point
OA	= Fixed costs
DE	= Loss at production point D (below breakeven)
FG	= Profit at production point G (above breakeven)
OA ÷ OB	= Contribution margin
FG ÷ BG	= Contribution margin

Focus on

Planning, Control, and Analysis—Module 47

Joint Products and By-products

Joint Product Costing

Joint products—two or more products resulting from same process

- **Joint product costs**—costs incurred before products separated
- **Split-off point**—earliest point at which products can be separated
- **Sales value**—amount each product can be sold for at earliest point of sale
- **Separable costs**—costs incurred after split-off point before products can be sold
- **Relative sales value**—Sales value—Separable costs

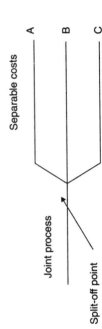

Separable costs

A

B

C

Joint process

Split-off point

Joint Product Costing (continued)

Allocating joint product costs—relative sales value method

1. Calculate relative sales value for each joint product
2. Add together to calculate total relative sales value
3. Calculate ratio of relative sales value for each joint product to total relative sales value
4. Multiply ratio for each product by joint product costs
5. Result is amount of joint product costs to be allocated to each product

Accounting for By-Products

Revenues from sale of by-product generally reduce cost of other products

1. Determine revenues from sale of by-products

2. Reduce by separable costs, if any, and costs of disposal

3. Net amount reduces cost of primary product or joint costs

Focus on

Planning, Control, and Analysis—Module 47

Product and Service Pricing

Factors that affect price of product or service:

- Cost of manufacturing and delivering product or cost of delivering service
- Quality of product or service
- Life of product
- Customers' preferences as to quality or price

Pricing Models

Profit based on sales price

Sales price	100%
Cost	100% − Profit %
Gross profit	Profit %

Profit based on cost

Sales price	100% + Profit %
Cost	100%
Gross profit	Profit %

INDEX

Index

173

Index